Musician's Practice Journal
by INCREDIBLY USEFUL NOTEBOOKS

The Musician's Practice Journal, *for all musicians*
Copyright © 2015 Incredibly Useful Notebooks.

www.incrediblyusefulnotebooks.com

Musician's Practice Journal

by INCREDIBLY USEFUL NOTEBOOKS

Practice Journal

WEEKLY FOCUS

DAY Monday

DAY Tuesday

DAY Wednesday

		Practice Journal

DAY	Thursday			DAY	Friday		

DAY	Saturday			DAY	Sunday		

NOTES

Practice Journal

WEEKLY FOCUS

DAY Monday

DAY Tuesday

DAY Wednesday

DAY	Thursday			DAY	Friday		

DAY	Saturday			DAY	Sunday		

NOTES

Practice Journal

WEEKLY FOCUS

DAY	Monday		

DAY	Tuesday		

DAY	Wednesday		

DAY	Thursday			DAY	Friday		

DAY	Saturday			DAY	Sunday		

NOTES

Practice Journal

WEEKLY FOCUS

DAY	Monday		

DAY	Tuesday			DAY	Wednesday		

Practice Journal

DAY	Thursday			DAY	Friday		

DAY	Saturday			DAY	Sunday		

NOTES

Practice Journal

WEEKLY FOCUS

DAY   Monday

DAY   Tuesday

DAY   Wednesday

DAY	Thursday			DAY	Friday		

DAY	Saturday			DAY	Sunday		

NOTES

Practice Journal

WEEKLY FOCUS

DAY	Monday		

DAY	Tuesday		

DAY	Wednesday		

DAY	Thursday		

DAY	Friday		

DAY	Saturday		

DAY	Sunday		

NOTES

Practice Journal

WEEKLY FOCUS

DAY Monday

DAY Tuesday

DAY Wednesday

Practice Journal

DAY	Thursday			DAY	Friday		

DAY	Saturday			DAY	Sunday		

NOTES

Practice Journal

WEEKLY FOCUS

DAY	Monday		

DAY	Tuesday		

DAY	Wednesday		

		Practice Journal

DAY	Thursday			DAY	Friday		

DAY	Saturday			DAY	Sunday		

NOTES

Practice Journal

WEEKLY FOCUS

DAY Monday

DAY Tuesday

DAY Wednesday

			Practice Journal

DAY	Thursday			DAY	Friday		

DAY	Saturday			DAY	Sunday		

NOTES

Practice Journal

WEEKLY FOCUS

DAY   Monday

DAY   Tuesday

DAY   Wednesday

DAY	Thursday			DAY	Friday		

DAY	Saturday			DAY	Sunday		

NOTES

Practice Journal

WEEKLY FOCUS

DAY	Monday		

DAY	Tuesday		

DAY	Wednesday		

Practice Journal

DAY	Thursday			DAY	Friday		

DAY	Saturday			DAY	Sunday		

NOTES

Practice Journal

WEEKLY FOCUS

DAY   Monday

DAY   Tuesday

DAY   Wednesday

Practice Journal

DAY	Thursday			DAY	Friday		

DAY	Saturday			DAY	Sunday		

NOTES

Practice Journal

WEEKLY FOCUS

DAY	Monday		

DAY	Tuesday		

DAY	Wednesday		

			Practice Journal

DAY	Thursday			DAY	Friday		

DAY	Saturday			DAY	Sunday		

NOTES

Practice Journal

WEEKLY FOCUS

DAY Monday

DAY Tuesday

DAY Wednesday

			Practice Journal

DAY	Thursday			DAY	Friday		

DAY	Saturday			DAY	Sunday		

NOTES

Practice Journal

WEEKLY FOCUS

DAY	Monday		

DAY	Tuesday		

DAY	Wednesday		

DAY	Thursday			DAY	Friday		

DAY	Saturday			DAY	Sunday		

NOTES

Practice Journal

WEEKLY FOCUS

DAY	Monday		

DAY	Tuesday		

DAY	Wednesday		

				Practice Journal

DAY	Thursday			DAY	Friday		

DAY	Saturday			DAY	Sunday		

NOTES

Practice Journal

WEEKLY FOCUS

DAY   Monday

DAY   Tuesday

DAY   Wednesday

Practice Journal

DAY	Thursday			**DAY**	Friday		

DAY	Saturday			**DAY**	Sunday		

NOTES

Practice Journal

WEEKLY FOCUS

| DAY | Monday | | |

| DAY | Tuesday | | | DAY | Wednesday | | |

DAY	Thursday			DAY	Friday		

DAY	Saturday			DAY	Sunday		

NOTES

Practice Journal

WEEKLY FOCUS

DAY   Monday

DAY   Tuesday

DAY   Wednesday

DAY	Thursday			DAY	Friday		

DAY	Saturday			DAY	Sunday		

NOTES

Practice Journal

WEEKLY FOCUS

DAY   Monday

DAY   Tuesday

DAY   Wednesday

DAY	Thursday			DAY	Friday		

DAY	Saturday			DAY	Sunday		

NOTES

Practice Journal

WEEKLY FOCUS

DAY   Monday

DAY   Tuesday

DAY   Wednesday

Practice Journal

DAY	Thursday			DAY	Friday		

DAY	Saturday			DAY	Sunday		

NOTES

Practice Journal

WEEKLY FOCUS

DAY Monday

DAY Tuesday

DAY Wednesday

DAY	Thursday			DAY	Friday		

DAY	Saturday			DAY	Sunday		

NOTES

Practice Journal

WEEKLY FOCUS

DAY Monday

DAY Tuesday

DAY Wednesday

DAY	Thursday			DAY	Friday		

DAY	Saturday			DAY	Sunday		

NOTES

Practice Journal

WEEKLY FOCUS

DAY Monday

DAY Tuesday

DAY Wednesday

DAY	Thursday			DAY	Friday		

DAY	Saturday			DAY	Sunday		

NOTES

Practice Journal

WEEKLY FOCUS

DAY   Monday

DAY   Tuesday

DAY   Wednesday

DAY	Thursday			DAY	Friday		

DAY	Saturday			DAY	Sunday		

NOTES

Practice Journal

WEEKLY FOCUS

DAY	Monday		

DAY	Tuesday			DAY	Wednesday		

DAY	Thursday			DAY	Friday		

DAY	Saturday			DAY	Sunday		

NOTES

Practice Journal

WEEKLY FOCUS

DAY   Monday

DAY   Tuesday

DAY   Wednesday

Practice Journal

DAY	Thursday			DAY	Friday		

DAY	Saturday			DAY	Sunday		

NOTES

Practice Journal

WEEKLY FOCUS

DAY Monday

DAY Tuesday

DAY Wednesday

DAY	Thursday			DAY	Friday		

DAY	Saturday			DAY	Sunday		

NOTES

Practice Journal

WEEKLY FOCUS

DAY	Monday		

DAY	Tuesday		

DAY	Wednesday		

Practice Journal

DAY	Thursday			DAY	Friday		

DAY	Saturday			DAY	Sunday		

NOTES

Practice Journal

WEEKLY FOCUS

DAY   Monday

DAY   Tuesday

DAY   Wednesday

Practice Journal

DAY	Thursday			DAY	Friday		

DAY	Saturday			DAY	Sunday		

NOTES

Practice Journal

WEEKLY FOCUS

DAY Monday

DAY Tuesday

DAY Wednesday

DAY	Thursday			DAY	Friday		

DAY	Saturday			DAY	Sunday		

NOTES

Practice Journal

WEEKLY FOCUS

DAY	Monday		

DAY	Tuesday			DAY	Wednesday		

DAY	Thursday			DAY	Friday		

DAY	Saturday			DAY	Sunday		

NOTES

Practice Journal

WEEKLY FOCUS

DAY	Monday		

DAY	Tuesday		

DAY	Wednesday		

DAY	Thursday			DAY	Friday		

DAY	Saturday			DAY	Sunday		

NOTES

Practice Journal

WEEKLY FOCUS

DAY	Monday		

DAY	Tuesday		

DAY	Wednesday		

DAY	Thursday			DAY	Friday		

DAY	Saturday			DAY	Sunday		

NOTES

Practice Journal

WEEKLY FOCUS

DAY	Monday		

DAY	Tuesday		

DAY	Wednesday		

DAY	Thursday			DAY	Friday		

DAY	Saturday			DAY	Sunday		

NOTES

Practice Journal

WEEKLY FOCUS

DAY	Monday		

DAY	Tuesday			DAY	Wednesday		

DAY	Thursday			DAY	Friday		

DAY	Saturday			DAY	Sunday		

NOTES

Practice Journal

WEEKLY FOCUS

DAY Monday

DAY Tuesday

DAY Wednesday

DAY	Thursday			DAY	Friday		

DAY	Saturday			DAY	Sunday		

NOTES

Practice Journal

WEEKLY FOCUS

DAY   Monday

DAY   Tuesday

DAY   Wednesday

			Practice Journal

DAY	Thursday			**DAY**	Friday		

DAY	Saturday			**DAY**	Sunday		

NOTES

Practice Journal

WEEKLY FOCUS

DAY   Monday

DAY   Tuesday

DAY   Wednesday

		Practice Journal

DAY	Thursday			DAY	Friday		

DAY	Saturday			DAY	Sunday		

NOTES

Practice Journal

WEEKLY FOCUS

DAY   Monday

DAY   Tuesday

DAY   Wednesday

Practice Journal

DAY	Thursday			DAY	Friday		

DAY	Saturday			DAY	Sunday		

NOTES

Practice Journal

WEEKLY FOCUS

DAY   Monday

DAY   Tuesday

DAY   Wednesday

				Practice Journal

DAY	Thursday			DAY	Friday		

DAY	Saturday			DAY	Sunday		

NOTES

Practice Journal

WEEKLY FOCUS

DAY Monday

DAY Tuesday

DAY Wednesday

| | | | Practice Journal |

DAY	Thursday			DAY	Friday		

DAY	Saturday			DAY	Sunday		

NOTES

Practice Journal

WEEKLY FOCUS

DAY	Monday		

DAY	Tuesday		

DAY	Wednesday		

Practice Journal

DAY	Thursday			DAY	Friday		

DAY	Saturday			DAY	Sunday		

NOTES

Practice Journal

WEEKLY FOCUS

DAY Monday

DAY Tuesday

DAY Wednesday

			Practice Journal

DAY	Thursday			DAY	Friday		

DAY	Saturday			DAY	Sunday		

NOTES

Practice Journal

WEEKLY FOCUS

DAY	Monday	

DAY	Tuesday	

DAY	Wednesday	

DAY	Thursday			DAY	Friday		

DAY	Saturday			DAY	Sunday		

NOTES

Sample Journal Entry

Practice Journal	Page #	NAME or Week ending or Month

WEEKLY FOCUS

Learn new piece...
Memorize first section
Practice scales slowly - 3 octaves
Watch tone & touch
(...Posture !)

DAY	Monday	Tempo or Page #	Time
Major scales (three octaves) & Arpeggios in C, F#		96	*20 min*
Practice first section of new piece		60	*1.5 hrs*
Replay: song #5		84	*10 min*
remember to order new music later!			
Start tmrw @		76	*2 hours*

DAY	Tuesday			DAY	Wednesday	

Sample Journal Entry

Student's Name or Other Notes		**Page #**			Practice Journal

DAY 2/10 Thursday	*Page*	*Duration*	**DAY** *02/29/2024* Friday	*Time*	needs more work?
Warm-ups	*p. 21*	1:20	*Scale in F#*	12 min	no
			Tune One	15 min	yes
Method book Four	*p. 29*	1:00	*Arpeggios in C*	15 min	no
			Tune Two	17 min	no
			Section One Slow	10 min	yes
Method book Six	*p. 64*	0:40	*Section Two Slow*	26 min	maybe
			Full from memory	25 min	no
			Scales in F#	10 min	no
Productive Y/N:	*yes!*	*03:00*			

DAY Saturday			**DAY** Sunday		

NOTES *Find a recording of the new piece...*

Teacher's Name, Location, Time, and/or Lesson Notes

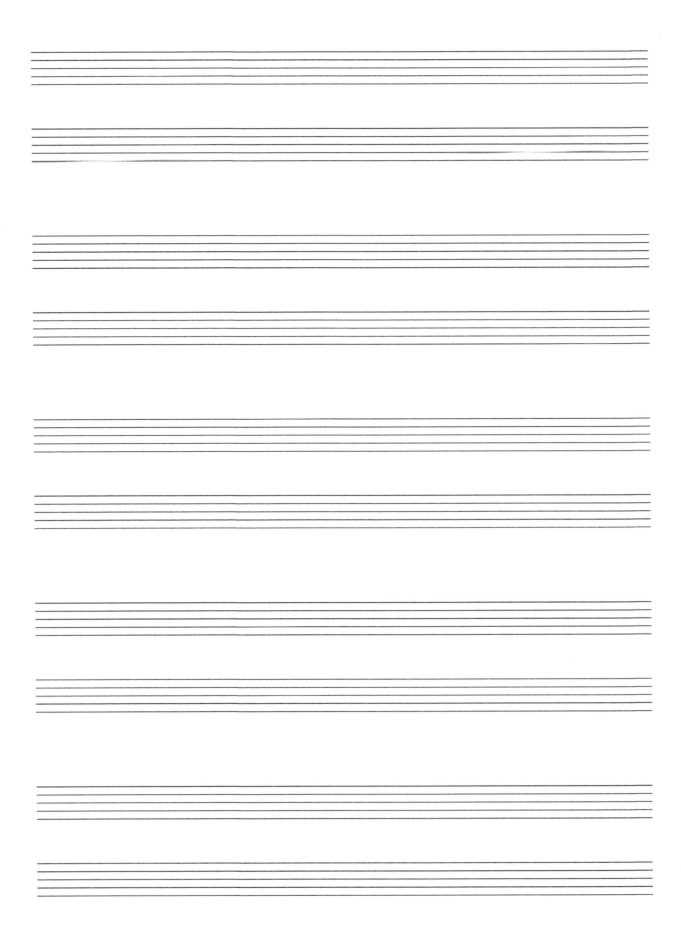

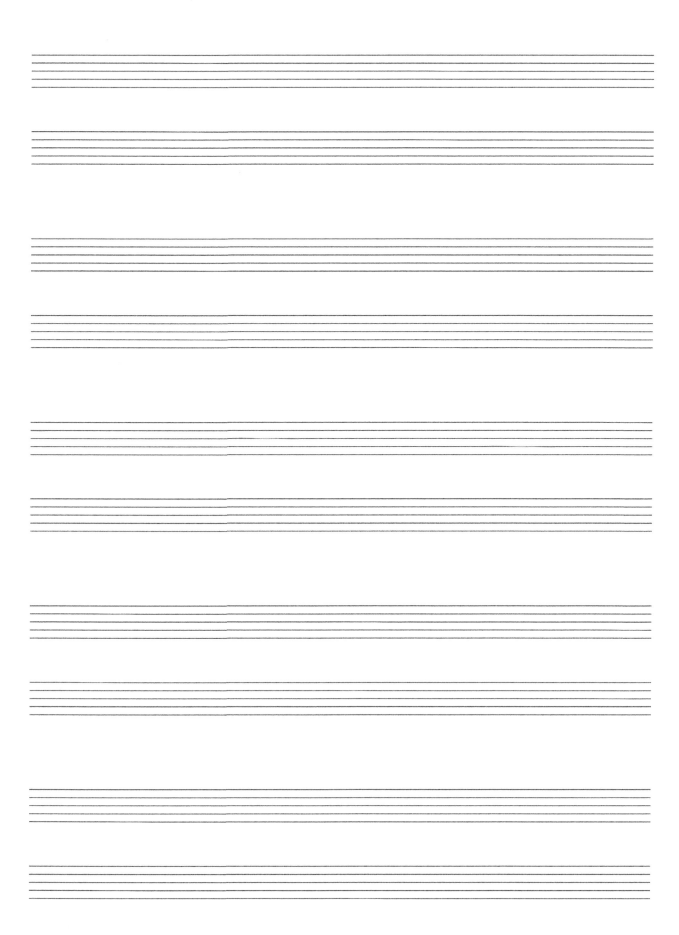

Made in the USA
Las Vegas, NV
28 February 2024

86429756R00057